MORE ADVENTURES OF THE SUPERKIDS

BY PLEASANT T. ROWLAND

ILLUSTRATED BY
MERYL HENDERSON
LORETTA LUSTIG
DOUG ROY
GARY UNDERCUFFLER

CONTRIBUTING WRITERS
SHIRLEYANN COSTIGAN
ANNE MARTIN
DONNA STAPLES
VALERIE TRIPP

ROWLAND READING FOUNDATION
MIDDLETON, WISCONSIN

ISBN 978-1-59833-507-1   MO33507.0613   3 4 5 6 7 8 9 10 WC 16 15 14 13

Table of Contents

Unit 1
In Case of Rain 6

⭐ by
   dry
   try

⭐ drizzly   messy
   funny   nifty
   happy   plenty
   hungry   rainy
   Icky   really
   Lily   sleepy

☆ day
   lay
   play
   say

down   too   work   many   first

paper   scissors   boots

⭐ When a word ends in *y* and it's the only vowel, the *y* stands for the long *i* sound.
⭐ When a word ends in *y* and has another vowel that is not next to it, the *y* stands for the long *e* sound.
☆ When a word has two vowels together, the first vowel is usually long and the second is silent.

In Case of Rain

One drizzly day, the Superkids made up games and projects to do inside. Work on one the next time it is too rainy to play outside.

Rainy Day Projects

From Superkids' Brains

A Monster Mask
by Tic and Cass

You Will Need:

a paper bag

paint

scissors

paper

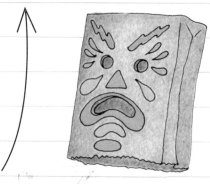

1. Make a mask by cutting holes in a paper bag, like this: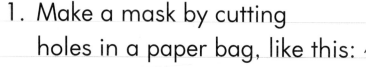

2. Paint the mask.
3. Tape paper teeth and funny ears to the mask.
4. Cut flaps on the sides of the bag and bend them back.

Put on the mask and act like a monster!

Leapfrog
by Sal, Tac, and Alf

You Will Need:
plenty of kids

1. Tell the kids to line up
   and scrunch down.
2. Go to the end of the line.
3. Jump like a frog over
   each person.
4. After you jump over the
   first person in line,
   scrunch down, too.
5. Tell the last person in line to
   jump over each kid and then
   scrunch down at the front
   of the line.
6. Play until each kid has hopped
   over the rest of the kids.

Teach leapfrog to your pals!

9

Odd Socks
by Oswald and Ettabetta

You Will Need:
one sock for each kid
many things with odd
    shapes that will fit in
    the socks

1. Put one thing in each sock.
2. Ask your pals to sit.
3. Hand each kid a sock.
   Say, "No peeking!"
4. Ask your pals to feel the
   socks and try to name what
   is in them.

A Doll's Rain Suit
by Doc

You Will Need:
a plastic sandwich bag
a doll
a safety pin
tape
scissors

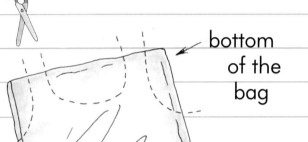

bottom of the bag

1. Cut three holes in a plastic sandwich bag.
2. Put it on the doll.
3. Pin one scrap of plastic on the doll's hair for a rain hat.
4. Tape the other plastic scraps on the doll's feet for rain boots.

Leaf Prints
by Frits and Lily

You Will Need:
a leaf
a flat stick
a brush
paint
paper

1. Lay the leaf on the paper.
2. Dip the brush in the paint.
3. Pick up the brush and
   the stick. Aim at the paper,
   like this:
4. Rub the stick across the
   brush. This is messy,
   but really fun.

5. Peel the leaf off the paper.
6. Let the paint dry.

Leaf prints make nifty gifts.

Feed Beanbags to a Dragon
by Icky and Hot Rod

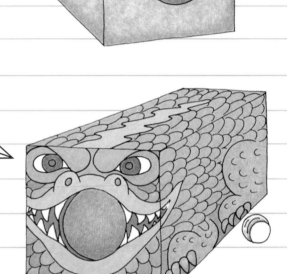

You Will Need:

a big box · five beanbags

paint · scissors

1. Cut a hole in a big box.
2. Paint a hungry dragon on it,
   like this:
3. Get five beanbags.
4. Pick two teams. Have three
   kids on each team.
5. Make a line three feet from
   the dragon.

How to Play:
The first kid on one team
stands at the line and
tosses five beanbags
at the dragon.

Keep track of how many bags
go in the hole.

Next, a kid from the other
team tosses beanbags at
the dragon. Keep going until
every kid has had a try. The
team that feeds the biggest
number of beanbags to the
dragon wins.

15

Sweet Dreams
by Toc

Lie down and sing this sleepy song.

Dream of good things:
Like buttercup tea,
And a boat that floats,
And a peppermint tree,
And a ride on the wings of a bumblebee,
And feeling as happy as you can be.

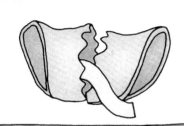

Unit 2
The Wish 18

er   est
easier   hungriest
happier   luckiest
sleepier   windiest

their   now   always   because   been

fortune cookie

The Wish

Chapter 1

Oswald wanted to run, but he was loaded down.

"Look at the lake!" he said. "I can't wait to jump in!"

"Last one in the lake is a rotten fish!" yelled Ettabetta.

The kids dived into the lake and splashed until Gus yelled, "Lunch!"

"Let's go!" said Sal. "I am the hungriest I have ever been! I think I could eat a whale!"

The kids ate their lunches. Then Lily passed a box of cookies.

"Take a fortune cookie," said Lily. "Your fortune is inside."

Doc's fortune said,

A person with freckles brings you luck.

"That is me!" said Cass with a grin.

"This is fun," said Hot Rod.
His fortune said,

Run and sing and always be glad.

"I like that," said Hot Rod.

Oswald's fortune said,

This is your lucky day.
You will get your wish.

"Your fortune is the luckiest, Oswald!"
said Ettabetta. "Quick, make a wish."

"I can't think of one now," said Oswald.
"I will save it."

"O.K.," said Ettabetta.

Chapter 2

After lunch, Oswald and Ettabetta looked
at the boats.

"I have never been on a boat," said Oswald.
"I wish I could go sailing."

"<u>That</u> is your wish!" said Ettabetta. "I hope you
will get it. We don't have a boat. But you could
float on an inner tube."

Ettabetta jumped into the lake. Oswald floated on an inner tube. He felt sleepier and sleepier. Then he fell asleep.

After a while, the kids began
to pack up their things because
it was time to go.

Suddenly Ettabetta yelled,
"Look! Oswald is out there
in the middle of the lake!"

The kids screamed and yelled. But Oswald couldn't hear them because he was asleep.

"Screech! Screech!" screamed a gull. It dived near the inner tube.

SPLASH!

Oswald woke up.

Chapter 3

"Oh, no!" he said. "How will I get back? My fortune said this was my lucky day. But just look at the mess I am in now!" He yelled, "Help! Help!"

"Look!" said Ettabetta. "A girl is sailing a boat near Oswald. I think she will pick him up."

The girl sailed the boat up to
Oswald. She reached down
and pulled him onto the boat.

At last, Oswald was safe.

"Thanks," he said to the girl.

"I am glad I could help you,"
she said. "But I need a hand now
because this is the windiest day
of the year. It will be easier to sail
the boat if you help me."

"O.K.," said Oswald.

The girl gave Oswald a life vest and a rope.
Oswald put on the vest and held on to
the rope. The wind filled the sails.
Oswald felt much happier.
It was terrific to be sailing.
He did not want the trip to end.

When the boat landed on the beach,
Oswald hopped out and thanked the girl.
Ettabetta ran up to him.

"Oswald," she said. "Your wish came true!"

"Yes," said Oswald. "This really was
my luckiest day!"

Trickers	Contractions			
baby	he'll	he's	I'm	we're
crazy	I'll	she's		
over	we'll	it's		
pony				
shady				
super				
tiny				

dark   picture

We made this album after a fun trip to Happy Land. We hope you'll have as much fun reading it as we had making it!

Icky

Lily

Doc

Hot Rod

Oswald

Tac

Alf

Sal!

Toc

Frits

Tic

CASS

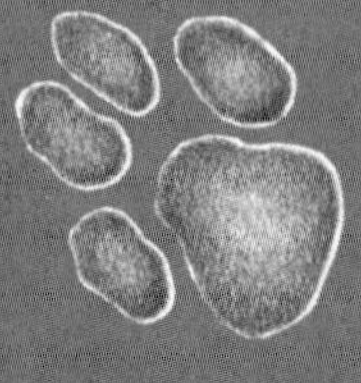

Ettabetta

A Super Day at Happy Land

One day Gus and Gert drove
us to Happy Land. Gert snapped
this picture of us when we got there.

It was Kids' Day at Happy Land.
Kids could get in free! We couldn't
wait to go on the rides.

Frits and Doc went on a ride named
Down the River. The boat went to the
top of a steep hill. Zip! Down it came.
SPLASH! Doc and Frits got wet. Doc
said she and Frits liked it!

Sal hit five empty bottles.
The man gave him a fluffy,
pink monster doll.

Lily, Toc, and Icky tried to tip over
the bottles. But the kids couldn't
hit very many. Their prizes were
just junky little hats.

35

This is us in the Monster Tunnel.
We couldn't see very well
because it was dark.
We were afraid.

Some of the kids liked the Animal Shed
at Happy Land the best. There were
baby goats, sheep, rabbits, ducks,
a mule, and a pony. The animal we
liked best was this itty-bitty tiny piggy.
We named her Taffy. Isn't she sweet?

Hot Rod and Ettabetta got stuck at
the top of the Ferris wheel. Hot Rod
couldn't look down. It was not fun to
be stuck up there. We cheered when
Hot Rod and Ettabetta got down.

We stopped to get hot dogs for lunch.

We sat on the grass under a big, shady oak tree. It was fun to look at the people passing by as we ate. The hot dogs were yummy, too!

38

Golly spotted a speaking trash can.
It said, "My name is Cubby.
Feed your trash to me."

Alf fed Cubby some trash.
SWISH! Cubby ate it.

Golly liked that trick!

Cass got a fluffy ball
of cotton candy. It was
sticky and sweet.

After lunch, we made Gus and Gert go on the Lucky Ducky. Gus and Gert looked very silly sitting with little kids. We couldn't stop giggling at them!

Tac and Oswald went on the Twist-Up and got too dizzy to stand up. Those two just kept giggling and acting crazy.

This is The Streak. It's the fastest ride in Happy Land. We waited and waited in line. At last we got on. We were off, lickety-split! We went up and down the hills as fast as the wind. We screamed a lot! We had so much fun, we went on The Streak another time.

At last it was time to go home.
Gert snapped this picture of us
on the way back. We'll remember
this super day for a long time!

Unit 4

Play Ball! 44
Rex King's Visit 52

<u>aw</u>	<u>all</u>
awful	all
awning	ball
Hawks	basketball
paws	call
saw	mall
	small
	tall

come   coming   they   our   put

Play Ball!

One day, the Superkids went to the shopping mall to get a new basketball. As they left the shop, Lily saw this:

Basketball Fans!
The Super Hawks are coming
to play basketball in the mall.

"Look!" said Lily. "The Super Hawks are coming. They are the best basketball team. Come on. Let's go see them!"

44

"Let's all sit on this bench," said Cass.
"So we'll be close to the players."

"I like the Super Hawks," said Sal.
"They're good players."

Just then the Super Hawks began playing.

Number 2 passed the ball to Number 4. He shot it into the basket. SWISH! The Superkids clapped and yelled.

Number 6 got the ball. He shot it under the legs of Number 9. All the Superkids smiled.

Then Number 7 dribbled the ball as he ran. But he tripped and fell. The basketball popped from his hands. Up, up, up it went. It got stuck on top of the mall!

Lily ran to Number 7. "Can I help you up?" she asked.

"Thanks, I am O.K.," said Number 7. "But I just lost our basketball!"

"Your ball is stuck up there," said Lily. "But you can play with our new ball. The Superkids just got it at the mall."

"What is a Superkid?" asked Number 7.

"<u>We're</u> the Superkids!" yelled the Superkids.

"Will the Superkids play basketball with us?" asked Number 7.

"But basketball players are tall," said Lily. "We're small. We can't play basketball with you."

"Yes, you can!" said Number 7. He picked up Lily.

"I'm super tall!" said Lily. "I can be a basketball player."

The rest of the Super Hawks picked up the other Superkids.

"Play ball!" said Number 7.

"Play ball!" said Lily.

51

Rex King's Visit

"Look at this," said Hot Rod. "Rex
King is coming to visit. He'll pick the
winner of the Grand Land Contest."
"To win, your land has to look grand—
no litter," said Hot Rod.

"I never miss the Rex King Show on TV,"
said Tic.

"I like his show best of all," said Cass.

"What if Rex King comes past our bus?"
asked Hot Rod. "We have a lot of litter.
It looks awful. What will he think of us?"

"He'll think we are lazy Litter Critters,"
said Oswald.

"Let's fix things up before Rex King comes,"
said Tic. "Then maybe we can win the
Grand Land Contest."

Tic, Tac, and Toc helped Oswald
pick up trash. Frits cut the grass.
Alf and Doc scrubbed the bus.
Ettabetta hung a planter and
Icky put plants in it. Sal put up an
awning. Lily and Cass put a bench
under the awning.

"Our bus looks like new," said
Oswald. "What will we get if we
win the contest?"

"The winners get to be on TV with
Rex King," said Hot Rod.

Just then Lily saw a big van.
"Look!" she yelled. "It's the TV van!
Rex King is coming!"

The van stopped and a little man
stepped off. He was all glittery.

"Is that Rex King?" asked Oswald.

"He has freckles, just like me,"
said Cass.

"He looks better on TV,"
whispered Tic.

56

Rex King asked the kids, "Did you all
fix up this spot?"

Alf said, "Yup! We all did!"

"Well, my golly! It looks grand," said Rex.

Golly jumped up to kiss Rex.

"No, Golly," Cass said. "Rex didn't
call you."

"All my fans would like to get a look at this grand spot," said Rex. "You must be on TV with me. Yes, my golly, you win the Grand Land Contest."

"Yup! Yup!" said Golly.

Rex and his helpers set up for the show.

Then the show began. Rex King said lots of grand things. He handed Alf a silver cup for all the Superkids.

"This silver cup is for the winners of
the Grand Land Contest," he said.
"You did a grand job fixing up
your bus. My golly, yes."

At that, Golly jumped up.
He put his paws on Rex and
kissed him on the chin.

"Well, my golly!" said Rex.
"Isn't this grand? My golly!"

"Yup! Yup!" yapped Golly.

Unit 5

<u>ar</u>	<u>or</u>	<u>er</u>	<u>ir</u>	<u>ur</u>
alarm	for	disaster	girl	burn
car	morning	discovered	Mirandez	burning
Carmen	reporter	ladder		fur
department	Salvador	rivers		hurry
harder	storm	scattered		returning
marching		shiver		Thursday
star		terrific		turned
Vargas		thunder		
		yesterday		

cold   know   does   laugh   both   again

adventure   fire chief   firefighters   telephone

Fire!

Chapter 1

RING! RING!

Chief Flinn picked up the telephone.
"Fire Department Number Six," he said.
"What? I don't speak Spanish. Wait!"

"Does anybody know how to speak
Spanish?" yelled the fire chief.

"I know Spanish," said Sal.

"Good," said the chief. "Come
and speak to this girl."

Sal spoke to the girl in Spanish. Then he said to the chief, "She says there is a fire on White Street!"

The fire chief rang the alarm. The firefighters came running. They put on their hats and coats as they jumped on the fire truck.

People in the streets scattered as the truck rushed by.

"Come with me," the fire chief said to Sal. "I'll need your help."

Sal jumped into the red car with the chief and they sped off.

Chapter 2

As the car turned onto White
Street, Sal could see big puffs
of gray smoke. The red car
screeched to a stop.

"Let's go!" said the fire chief.
A little girl ran up to the chief.

"My mom! My dad! My sisters and brothers!" yelled the little girl in Spanish. "They are trapped!"

"Quick!" yelled Sal to the chief. "Her family is trapped upstairs!"

"Hurry. Get the ladder up!" yelled the chief.

¡Mi mamá! ¡Mi papá! ¡Mis hermanos! ¡Están arriba!

67

The big ladder went up, up, up.

Some of the firefighters helped the family come down the ladder. Other firefighters sprayed the flames with hoses.

At last the fire was out. The mom and dad thanked the fire chief again and again.

Chapter 3

Just then, a reporter for the <u>Morning Star</u> came.

"Is the fire out?" asked the reporter.

"Yes!" said the chief. "And everyone is safe."

"Good!" said the reporter. "It looks like you and your firefighters saved the day."

"We had a lot of help," said Chief Flinn. "Without Sal and Carmen, the fire would have been a real disaster. They are the real stars of this adventure."

"That is terrific," said the reporter. "Tell me about it."

Sal and Carmen both spoke to the reporter. Sal explained what Carmen said in Spanish.

The next day, the front of the <u>Morning Star</u> looked like this:

MORNING

Sunny and hot today

FAMILY IS SAVED FROM BURNING HOME

Two Kids Help Fire Department

A fire broke out yesterday in the home of the Vargas family at 19 White Street. Carmen Vargas discovered the fire. The rest of the family was trapped upstairs.

Thursday, June 18

Carmen quickly called the Fire Department. Luckily, Salvador Mirandez was visiting Fire Department 6 when Carmen called. Carmen speaks only Spanish. Salvador explained what Carmen was saying to the fire chief.

Fire Chief Flinn said, "Without the help of both those children, that fire would have been a disaster!"

It Is Hot

Gosh! It is hot!
Can't you see the street shimmer?
Don't you feel your skin simmer?
Does the pavement burn your feet?
Want to play?

I do not.
It is too hot.

74

Gosh! It is hot!
But we could sit in the shade
And pretend a parade
Is marching down the street.
Want to play?

I do not.
It is too hot.

Gosh! It is hot!
The sun seems to be humming.
No, a fire truck is coming.
Let's chase it down the street.
Want to play?

I do not.
It is too hot.

It is so hot.
The fire chief opened a pipe, see!
Now look! He is calling you and me!
There are rivers in the street!
Want to play?

I do!
Don't you?

The Super Hiding Spot

Chapter 1

The Superkids were playing hide-and-seek.
Tic was It. She called, "One, two, three,
four, five . . ." The kids all scattered to hide.
Toc hid under a big box. Alf hid behind
a bench. Frits hid behind a trash can.
Icky hid inside a big pipe.

"Here I come!" hollered Tic.

Icky laughed softly. He could hear Tic yell, "I see Frits hiding behind the trash can! I see Sal hiding up on a branch!"

"Their hiding spots aren't as good as mine," laughed Icky. "Tic will never discover me."

Icky waited. Tic came close to the pipe, but she didn't peek inside.

"She doesn't know where I am," Icky said to himself. "I'll wait here a little longer. I bet Tic will give up and then I'll win."

PING. PING. PING.

Rain began to fall on the pipe.

"Oh, no," said Icky. "Now I am stuck. I'll have to wait until the rain stops."

Chapter 2

Icky could hear the Superkids running home. Then all he could hear was the rain. Icky saw a flash in the sky. He put his hands over his ears and waited for the crash of thunder.

CRASH! CRACK! RUMBLE, RUMBLE, RUMBLE.

Icky began to shiver. He was cold and scared.

Suddenly a wet ball of fur shot into the pipe.

"Golly! You wet mutt! What are you doing here?" asked Icky.

Golly stared up at Icky with a sad look. He tried to sit on Icky's lap.

Thunder rumbled again and Golly shivered harder.

"Does the storm scare you?" Icky asked Golly. "It scares me a little bit, too. But you and I can be brave together."

Icky tried to look brave. Golly wagged his tail a little bit. Icky patted Golly's back and scratched his ears.

At last Golly wasn't shaking anymore. Icky smiled. He felt better, too. It was much easier to be brave when someone needed his help.

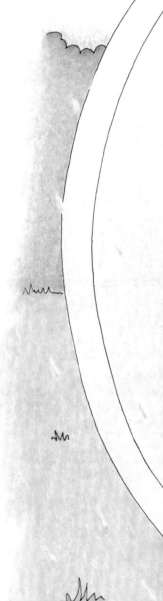

Chapter 3

When the rain and thunder stopped,
Icky could hear the kids returning.
Quickly, he and Golly dashed out of the pipe.

"One, two, three, all in free!" yelled Icky.

"Icky!" said Tic. "Where were you hiding
all this time?"

Icky smiled. "I had the best hiding spot of all,"
he said. "Only Golly knows where it was.
And Golly will never tell."

Unit 6

For the Birds 86
The Lost Mitt 101

<u>oi</u>

coins

disappointed

join

moist

pointed

soil

<u>oy</u>

annoy

boy

enjoy

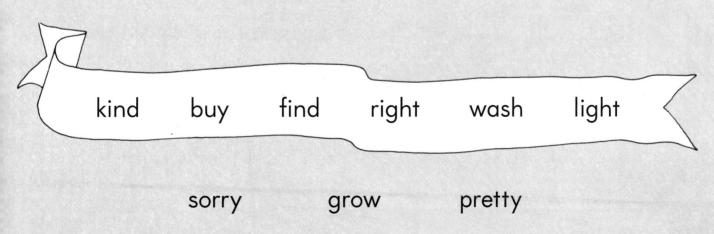

kind   buy   find   right   wash   light

sorry   grow   pretty

For the Birds

PLANT A GARDEN

Free garden plots!
You bring the seeds.
Come to Government Hall!

Chapter 1

"It would be fun to plant a garden," said Alf.

"Yes!" said Toc. "Let's ask the kids if they want to."

Alf and Toc ran to the bus.

"Who wants to plant a garden?" asked Toc.

"I do!" said all the kids.

"Terrific!" said Alf. "We just have to buy seeds."

Hot Rod said, "But I don't have any cash."

"We can use coins from the club bank," said Doc.

"Toc and I will get a garden plot," said Alf.
 "You kids go buy the seeds."

"O.K.," said the rest of the Superkids.

Alf and Toc ran to Government Hall. Lots of people were waiting to get garden plots.

"Let's join the line," said Alf.

Toc and Alf had to wait a long, long time.

At last it was their turn.
The gardener gave them
plot number four. She said,
"This plot gets plenty of light.
It's just right for you."

"Thank you!" said Alf and Toc.

They rushed back to the bus.

Chapter 2

"We got a plot!" said Alf and Toc. "Did you get seeds?"

Hot Rod said, "Yes! Tac and I got corn seeds. Oswald and Lily got carrot seeds. Ettabetta and Sal are planting beans."

"Peas for Tic and me," said Doc.

"Radishes for me!" yelled Frits.

"And beets for Icky and me!" said Cass.

"What kind of seeds did you get for Alf and me?" asked Toc.

"Oh, no!" said Doc. "We forgot you!"

"We're sorry," said Hot Rod.

Alf and Toc were disappointed. They had waited in line so long! "Well," said Toc. "You had better start planting without us."

So the other kids left.

"I wish we could buy seeds," said Toc. "But there is no cash left."

"My mom puts birdseed in our bird feeder," said Alf. "We could plant some of that. The birds won't miss it."

"Let's try it," said Toc.

Alf lifted Toc up. She grabbed a handful of birdseed.

Alf and Toc went to the garden.

Toc pointed to a spot in the back.
"Let's plant our seeds there,"
she said.

"O.K.," said Alf.

Chapter 3

"What are you planting?" asked Sal.

"Birdseed!" said Toc.

The kids laughed.

"Are you going to grow birds?"
giggled Tic.

"Tweet, tweet!" laughed Tac.

Toc and Alf ignored the kids.
They planted the birdseed.
They kept the soil moist.
Each day they checked to see
if the birdseed had started to grow.

"How is your tweet weed?"
laughed Cass.

"Do you have bird blossoms yet?"
giggled Icky.

"Those kids annoy me," said Toc.

"Me too!" said Alf. "I don't enjoy
their jokes."

Chapter 4

After a while, all the seeds began to grow. Carrots, radishes, corn, beans, peas, and beets started to pop up. Something even began to pop up from the birdseed!

Each day the birdseed plants got bigger.
In fact, they were the tallest plants in
the garden! The kids stopped making fun
of Alf and Toc. Then, on one sunny day,
the birdseed plants blossomed!

"That birdseed plant is so pretty!" said Doc.

"It's the best plant in the garden," said Tac.

"Thank you!" said Toc and Alf.

Just then a bird landed on the plant and began to sing. Toc laughed. She said, "See? We DID grow birds after all!"

The Lost Mitt

Chapter 1

"Frits, what a neat baseball mitt," Ettabetta said.

"Yes, it's pretty good," Frits said as he punched it.

"I have been saving to buy that kind of mitt," said Ettabetta. "But I still need more cash. I could really use a mitt today. My team has a big game."

"I'll lend you my mitt,"
said Frits.

"You will?" said Ettabetta.
"Oh, boy! Thanks, Frits."

Frits tossed the mitt to
Ettabetta and she grabbed it
with one hand.

"Good catch!" said Frits with
a laugh.

The kids played their ball game.
Ettabetta's team was winning.
Ettabetta punched Frits's mitt
and whispered, "Come on, mitt,
we can do it. Only one more
catch and we win the game."

WHAM! The batter hit the ball.
The ball went way up into the sky.

"Catch it!" yelled Ettabetta's team.

Ettabetta ran to the left, then back.
Then she stretched and held the mitt
up in the air.

THUD!

The ball landed right in the mitt. All the
kids clapped and cheered happily.

Chapter 2

Ettabetta was so happy, she tossed the mitt up in the air. It was the best game Ettabetta had ever played.

That evening, Ettabetta could hardly sleep. She kept seeing that last ball land in Frits's wonderful mitt. "I would never have won the game without Frits's mitt," she said to herself.

Suddenly, she sat up. "Frits's mitt!"
she said to herself. "Oh, no! I must have
left it at the ballpark. When it gets light,
I'll go look for it."

When the sun came up, Ettabetta went
to the ballpark. She looked everywhere for
the mitt. But she couldn't find it.

"This is awful," said Ettabetta. "Frits will be so mad. What can I do?"

Then she remembered her savings. "Maybe I can make some extra cash and buy Frits a new mitt! Maybe he won't even know that it is different."

Chapter 3

Ettabetta went to see if Gus and Gert had any jobs. They did. First she had to wash a car. Then she put out the trash. Then she washed more cars. By the end of the morning, she had made the cash she needed.

Ettabetta ran to the sports shop. She paid for the new mitt.

Ettabetta saw Frits at the bus.
She tossed the new mitt to him and
said, "Frits, your mitt was super.
Thanks a lot."

Frits looked surprised. He said,
"This is a pretty good mitt, Ettabetta.
But it's not mine."

Ettabetta gulped. "It is now,"
she said sadly. "I lost yours, so
I had to buy this one for you.
I'm sorry."

"But, Ettabetta," Frits said, "I have my mitt. Icky picked it up after the game. He gave it to me this morning."

"Really?" said Ettabetta.

"Really," said Frits. He tossed the new mitt to Ettabetta and grinned. "But now you have the mitt you wanted. Let's play catch!"

Unit 7

Trickers

<u>ar</u>	<u>or</u>	<u>ear</u>
backward	doctor	earth
dollars	word	heard
forward	work	learned
	working	

eyes   Mrs.   pretty

Slumber Party

Tic, Lily, and Cass set up a tent in Tic's backyard. "We'll have a slumber party," said Tic happily.

"It's fun to sleep in a tent," said Cass.

"Yes!" said Tic.

But Lily didn't say a word. This was the first time she had slept away from home, and she was sort of afraid.

The girls snuggled into their sleeping bags and began to whisper and giggle. It was very dark.

"I'll tell a story about a creepy monster," said Tic.

"Oh, no!" said Lily.

"Oh, yes!" said Cass.

"It's a good story," said Tic. "You'll like it." She began to tell it.

One day a boy was going down the road when he saw a pot full of silver dollars. "My mother will be happy when she sees this!" he said. He put the pot under his arm and ran home.

But the boy didn't know that the silver dollars belonged to a creepy monster! Later, when the boy went to sleep, the monster came to find him.

"Whooo stole my silver dollars?"
said the monster.

The boy heard him and woke up.
"I must be dreaming!" he said. But
the monster came closer.

"Whooo stole my silver dollars?"
the monster asked. The boy felt
something tapping his leg. "Whooo
stole my silver dollars? Was it YOU?"

Just as Tic said "YOU," she grabbed Lily.

"Eek!" screamed Lily.

"Yikes!" yelled Cass.

Then Tic and Cass laughed. But Lily
did not.

"I liked that story," said Cass.

Lily didn't say a word.

"Let's go to sleep," said Tic. The girls
snuggled into their sleeping bags.
It was very still and very dark.

Lily tried to sleep, but she just couldn't.
She kept thinking about Tic's story.

"Why did Tic tell that creepy story?" Lily
wondered. Suddenly, Lily felt something
wiggle by the bottom of her sleeping bag.

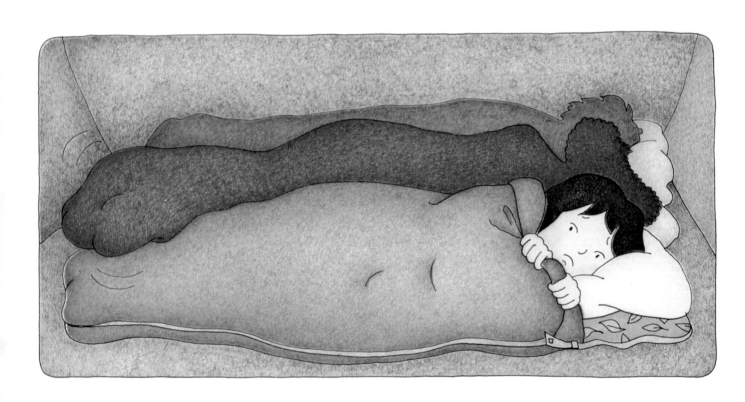

There was something down there!
It wiggled again. Lily screamed and
grabbed her sleeping bag.

"What is the matter?" said Tic. "Why are
you grabbing my feet?"

"Oh," said Lily. "Are those your feet?"
Suddenly, she couldn't keep back her tears.

"I'm afraid of the dark," Lily said.

"I was, too," said Tic. "But I learned a wonderful thing." She lifted the tent flaps. "Look," she said. Tic pointed to the sky.

Cass and Lily looked at the sky. It was full of stars.

"When it is dark, the stars shine in the sky. If you remember the stars are shining for you, then you won't be afraid," said Tic.

"I like the way the stars sparkle," said Lily. One big star seemed to wink at her. Lily smiled.

"Do you think you can
go to sleep now?" asked Tic.

"Yes," said Lily.
She felt much better.
In a little while, she
was fast asleep.

121

Making Stars

If the stars are hard to see where you are, you can make stars.

To make stars, you'll need an empty carton, a tack, and a flashlight.

First, poke holes in the bottom of the carton with the tack.

Next, turn on the flashlight and turn off all the other lights.

Then, put the flashlight in the carton and shine your stars up on the wall.

Last, turn your flashlight off and on again and again to make the stars wink and blink.

The Runaway Dragon

"Hot Rod," said Doc. "What is Oswald doing in the bus?"

"He's working on a project," said Hot Rod. "I think it's a surprise."

Suddenly, Oswald came running out of the bus with a little box.

He pushed a purple button on the box. "Stand back!" Oswald yelled.

Something came flying out of the bus. It had big flashing eyes and a horrible grin.

"A dragon!" gasped Doc.

The dragon dipped and dived.
Oswald could make it do
whatever he wanted it to do.
Oswald pushed a red button and
the dragon landed safely.

"How does it work?" asked Doc.

"There is a model plane inside
the dragon," said Oswald. "This
black box makes the plane work."

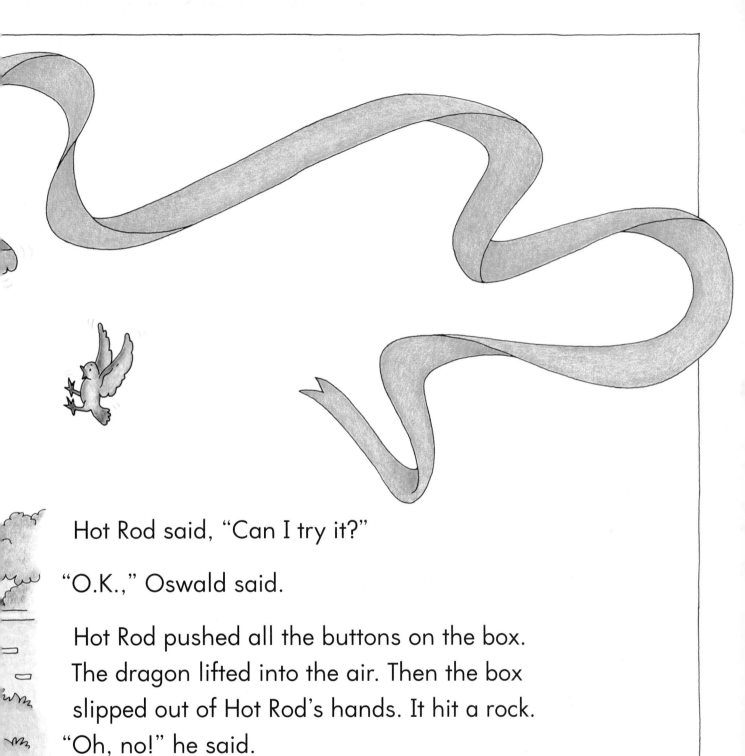

Hot Rod said, "Can I try it?"

"O.K.," Oswald said.

Hot Rod pushed all the buttons on the box. The dragon lifted into the air. Then the box slipped out of Hot Rod's hands. It hit a rock. "Oh, no!" he said.

Suddenly, the dragon dived at them.

Doc, Hot Rod, and Oswald ducked. Oswald pushed each button on the box. Nothing happened.

"It doesn't work!" cried Oswald. "We'll have to catch the dragon or it will crash!"

The kids ran, but they couldn't catch the fast dragon. It quickly zipped up over the trees. Its long green tail flapped in the wind. Then the kids couldn't see the dragon at all.

131

"What is happening?" asked Gus.

"I don't know," said Mrs. Dearing. "This big thing dived out of the sky at me. It looked like a DRAGON!"

Oswald, Doc, and Hot Rod came running down the street. They yelled, "Has anyone seen a dragon?"

Ben came running up. He said,
"Has anyone seen Polly, my parrot?
Something green came flying past
my shop. Polly cried, 'Oh, my pretty
bird.' Then she went flying after it."

"Oh, no," groaned Oswald.
  "Polly is chasing my paper dragon."

  Ben said, "Silly Polly!"

"Look!" said a little boy.
  "There they are!"

  Everyone looked up.

"My dragon!"
  said Oswald.

"My parrot!" cried Ben.

"Pretty bird!" squawked
  the parrot.

Up in the sky, the dragon and Polly
dipped and twirled. Down on the street,
Oswald and Ben ran to the left, then
forward, then backward.

Suddenly, the dragon started to
dive down.

"Oh, no!" Oswald cried. "My dragon is
going to crash!"

But Polly grabbed the dragon and held on to it. The dragon and the parrot landed with a soft thud.

"Oh, my silly dragon," said Oswald.

"Oh, my silly Polly!" laughed Ben.

"Oh, my pretty bird!" squawked Polly. "Oh my!"

Unit 8

The Lesson 138

That Was Yesterday 149

ou	ow = Ow!	ow = ō
about	crowd	show
around	crowded	window
counted	frowned	
found	how	
grouchy	now	
loudly	Powers	
our	scowled	
out	wow	
shouted		
sound		

warm   walk   give   once   done

house   Ms.

The Lesson

"Hot Rod has been to the bus only once this week," said Cass. "I wonder what he is doing."

Oswald said, "I just saw him. He wouldn't tell me where he was going. He was grouchy about it, too."

"Maybe he needs help," said Cass. "Let's find him."

Cass and Oswald found Hot Rod's bike in front of a house on Second Street. Cass asked, "What is Hot Rod doing in there?"

"Let's see," said Oswald. Cass and Oswald walked over to the house. They heard a tune coming from a window.

Bee bop ditty ditty wow wow,
Bee bop ditty ditty wonk wonk!

A woman inside said, "You made a mistake, Hot Rod. Play it again."

Bee bop ditty ditty wow wow,
Bee bop ditty ditty wonk wonk!

"Oh, no," said Hot Rod. "The clarinet is too hard, Ms. Powers. I want to quit."

Ms. Powers said, "Don't give up, Hot Rod. You are doing well. In fact, I want you to play in the talent show on Saturday."

"But I don't want to play anymore," said Hot Rod.

"Give it a try," said Ms. Powers. "If you still want to quit after the talent show, I will understand."

"Well, O.K.," said Hot Rod. "But I hope my pals don't come. I don't want them to make fun of me."

"Let's get out of here," whispered Cass.

Back at the bus, Cass said, "It is terrific that Hot Rod plays the clarinet. Let's go to the show to hear him."

"Let's get all the kids to go," said Oswald. "But let's not tell them about Hot Rod. It will be a surprise."

Saturday came at last. All the Superkids walked to the show.

First a little girl played the drums.

BANG! BANG! BLAM! BLAM!

Then a tall boy sang a song.

Sal yawned.

Ettabetta wiggled. "Why did you make us come?" she asked Cass.

"You'll see," said Cass.

Then two girls played trumpets.

Wop wop blat blat blat!

The hall was getting warm.
Alf began to squirm. "This is
boring," he whispered to Sal.

Just then, someone began to
play a jazzy tune.

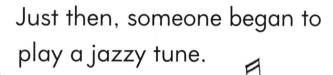
Bee bop ditty ditty wow wow,
Bee bop ditty ditty wow wow wow!

"It is Hot Rod!" said Icky. "I didn't
know he could play the clarinet!"

"He's really good!" said Doc.

The crowd snapped their fingers and tapped their feet. When Hot Rod was done, everyone clapped loudly.

After the show, Ms. Powers said, "Thank you, Hot Rod. You played very well. How do you feel about the clarinet now?"

"It's not so bad," said Hot Rod. "But I still want to give up my lessons."

Just then, the Superkids crowded around
Hot Rod. They all spoke at once.

Hot Rod, you're terrific!

Is it hard?

We didn't know you
could play the clarinet!

Show us how.

147

"Can you give me clarinet lessons, Hot Rod?" asked Cass.

"Yes," said Hot Rod. "But first I have to take more lessons myself! It feels good to play well, even if it takes time and hard work." He smiled at Ms. Powers and began to play.

♪ Bee bop ditty ditty wow wow,
Bee bop ditty ditty wow wee! ♫

That Was Yesterday

Chapter 1

The Superkids were playing tag.

"I'm It!" shouted Frits. He counted,
"1, 2, 3, 4, 5, 6, 7, 8, 9, 10! Look out!
Here I come!"

Alf ran past Frits. "You can't catch me!
You can't catch me!" teased Alf.

Frits chased Alf. When he got close, Frits reached out his hand. "I got you, Alf! You're It!" shouted Frits.

"I am not!" shouted Alf. "You missed me by a mile."

"I did not! I tagged you!" yelled Frits.

"You never came close," hollered Alf.

Alf and Frits began to push each other.

"Stop it!" said Doc.

"You'll get hurt!" said Hot Rod.

But Alf and Frits did not stop. The kids had to pull the two boys apart.

Ettabetta said, "Come on, you two.
Let's play tag."

"No! I quit!" said Frits as he stomped off.
"I'm not going to play tag with a cheater."

"I quit, too!" yelled Alf. "I'm going home."

The rest of the kids just sat there.

Sal said, "This is no fun. They have
spoiled the game for us, too."

"Let's just go," said Toc. The kids
split up and walked home.

Chapter 2

The next day the kids met at the bus. Frits and Alf frowned and scowled at each other.

"It is too warm to play tag," Toc said. "Let's go fishing!"

"Hurray!" shouted the kids.

Alf said, "I'm not going if Frits goes."

"And I'm not going if Alf goes," said Frits.

153

Toc was angry. "You spoiled our game yesterday," she said. "But you are not going to spoil our fishing trip. You can both just stay here!"

The kids left to go fishing. Frits and Alf were left on the bus alone.

"Now look what you did," said Alf.

"You started it," said Frits.

"I did not," said Alf.

"You did, too," said Frits.

"Oh, I wish you would just get out of here," grumbled Alf.

"I got here first!" shouted Frits.

"O.K., then stay. I don't care," said Alf.
He picked up a comic and began to read it.

Frits just stared out the window.

Chapter 3

For a long time Frits and Alf sat on the bus without making a sound.

Then Alf said softly, "Wow!"

Frits asked, "What?"

"Look at this!" said Alf. "This comic shows you how to make a skateboard!"

"Let me see!" said Frits. Alf handed him the comic. "Wow, that's terrific," said Frits.

"All you need is a board and some skates," said Alf.

Frits said, "I have skates we could use. Let's walk to my house and get them!"

"O.K.!" said Alf.

As Frits and Alf left the bus, they bumped into Sal.

"Where are you two going?" Sal asked.

"We're going to get my skates," said Frits.

"We're working on a super project," said Alf.

Sal said, "I didn't think you two were speaking."

Alf and Frits looked at each other. All at once they began to laugh.

"Well . . . that was yesterday," said Alf.

o͞o	o͝o
gloomy	books
room	good
soon	look
spooky	looked
too	took

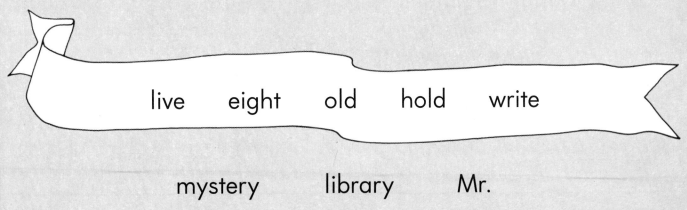

live   eight   old   hold   write

mystery   library   Mr.

The Case of the Mystery Monster

Lily took a pile of books to the checkout desk at the library.

"You must like mystery books," Mr. Burns said.

"Oh, yes," Lily said. "I do!"

"Well," said Mr. Burns. "You aren't the only one! Eight new mystery books are missing from the library."

"Who took them?" asked Lily.

"I have only one clue," Mr. Burns said. "I found this note."

The note said,

Hold on to your books!
The Mystery Monster lives here!

"Monster?" said Lily. "How could a monster live here?"

"I don't know," said Mr. Burns.

"Maybe I can help you," Lily said. "I will come every day and look for the Mystery Monster."

"Thank you, Lily," said Mr. Burns.

The next day, Lily went back to the library. "Hi, Mr. Burns," she said. "Did the Mystery Monster write any more notes?"

"No," said Mr. Burns. "But another book is missing!"

"Well," said Lily. "I'll sit next to the mystery shelf. Maybe the monster will come today."

Outside, the sky was gray and gloomy. Inside, the room was a bit dark and spooky. Lily turned on the lamp and settled down to read.

Lily peeked at people as they walked by her. But no one looked like a Mystery Monster.

Just then, Lily saw a man in a gray coat walk over to the mystery books. Lily slouched down in her seat and peeked at the man. "Is he the Mystery Monster?" she wondered.

The man just frowned at the mystery books. Then he walked over to the sports books.

"That man does not seem interested in mystery books," Lily said to herself.

Lily was hungry. She asked Mr. Burns, "May I go to lunch now?"

"Oh, yes," said Mr. Burns. "A spy needs a good lunch."

Lily walked to the window to check if it was raining. It wasn't, so she went to get her book. But her book had disappeared! On the table was a note:

Hold on to your books! The Mystery Monster lives here!

Lily whirled around. The man in the gray coat was walking quickly out of the library.

Lily ran over to Mr. Burns. "Mr. Burns!" she whispered. "Stop that man! He's the Mystery Monster!"

Mr. Burns looked surprised. He jumped up from his desk. Books went tumbling everywhere.

The man in the gray coat went outside.

"Oh, no," said Lily. "Now we will never catch the Mystery Monster!"

Mr. Burns looked very upset. "Oh, dear," he said. "Perhaps I let my little joke go too far. Let me show you something, Lily."

Mr. Burns took out a big sheet of paper from under his desk. It said:

Boys and Girls!
Coming Soon!
Mystery Book Week at the Library!
We'll have a Mystery Book Club and a Mystery Book Corner.
All Mystery Book Fans Invited.

The Mystery Monster

"You see, Lily," said Mr. Burns. "Mystery Book Week is coming in eight days. I took all the mystery books for the Mystery Corner. I was writing the notes myself."

"Oh, so you are the Mystery Monster," said Lily with a giggle.

"Yes," said Mr. Burns. "But now the surprise is spoiled for all the other boys and girls."

"No, it isn't," said Lily with a smile. "I won't tell. I can keep it to myself. After all, I enjoy a good mystery!"

Unit 10
Zoo Clue 172

soft c = s	soft g = j	Trickers with tag-along e
nice	gentle	figure
place	giraffe	giraffe
raced	huge	give
		have
		house
		live
		love
		please
		solve
		tease

Zoo Clue

"Where is Ettabetta?" asked Toc. "She asked us to meet her here at the zoo."

"Maybe she's inside," said Cass. "Let's find her."

The kids went up to the ticket booth.

"Are you the Superkids?" asked the lady in the booth.

"Yes," said Icky.

"I have something for you," said the lady. She handed a note to Icky.

Icky read it.

"Look!" said Hot Rod.
"The first riddle is on
the back."

I live in the desert.
I have a huge hump.
You can ride on my back.
I'm not a grump!

"It sounds like a camel!" said Frits.

"Yes! Let's find one," said Cass.

The Superkids went past the giraffes and the gorilla. A zookeeper let Doc feed a fish to a seal. The seal clapped happily. Then the kids found the camels.

"These camels are smiling," said Tic. "They aren't grumps."

"Just hungry!" laughed Frits.

"Look, here is another note,"
said Hot Rod.

I give milk,
And I say "moo."
I live on a farm,
But I'm here at the zoo.

"Goats give milk,"
said Oswald.

"But goats don't moo,"
said Lily. "Cows moo!"

"That's true," said Oswald.
"Let's find the cow."

The kids went past some goats.

"That little goat is super,"
said Tac.

"A little goat is called a kid,"
said Oswald.

"Then that little goat is a superkid!"
said Sal.

At last they came to a gentle cow. "Moo," said the cow.

"Moo to you, too," said Cass.

"Look, there is another note!" said Oswald.

Cass said, "Read it!"

I have two big ears
And a coat of brown.
I fly when it is dark,
And I hang upside down.

178

"A coat of brown means its fur is brown," said Oswald.

"If it has two big ears and brown fur, it could be a rabbit," said Sal.

"But rabbits don't fly," said Tac. "It must be a bird."

"But birds don't have big ears," said Toc.

"Owls look like they have ears. And they fly!" said Tac.

"But owls never hang upside down," said Icky. "Hold it! I know! It's a bat."

179

The kids raced to the bat house.
Inside, seven or eight bats were
flying around.

"I don't like this place," said Cass,
"Let's go!"

"Wait!" said Oswald.
"Ettabetta left another note."

This note is not a clue.
If you go to the Petting Zoo,
There will be a prize for you.
Ettabetta will be there, too.

"A prize!" said Hot Rod.
"Let's go!"

The Superkids ran to the
Petting Zoo.

181

"Where have you been?"
said Ettabetta.

"Some of your riddles
were tricky," said Tic.

I live in the desert.
I have a huge hump.
You can ride on my back.
I'm not a grump!

I give milk,
And I say "moo".
I live on a farm,
But I'm here at the zoo.

I have two big ears
And a coat of brown.
I fly when it is dark,
And I hang upside down.

"Where is our prize?" asked Hot Rod.

"You'll have to figure out what it is
first," said Ettabetta.

"Please don't tease us, Ettabetta!
We're tired," said Sal.

"Just look at the red letters in all the
clues," said Ettabetta. "Put them
together to make two words. The
words tell you what the prize is."